COMMUNITY ACTION PROJECTS
A Blueprint For Success

Author contact:
　　　Maria M. Shylov
　　　Maria@Shylov.com
　　　https://shylov.com
　　　www.facebook.com/EatWellFeelBetter

Cover design: Yuriy Shylov

Paperback **ISBN**: 9781080053674

Dedication

To my aunt, Mrs. Janja Veljkovic – my role model with a heart of gold, who taught me that no matter how hard our life can be, the kindness we give to others is the most memorable gift. Even now, while in her 80's, she actively looks for ways to help her community. She inspired me to help my community, encouraged me to be myself, to be tenacious and relentless when pursuing my dreams.

To my loving husband, thank you for being my rock and my sounding board.

To Dress for Success Vancouver and Dress for Success World-Wide – Thank you for selecting me to become a Dress for Success Delegate and for the opportunity to spearhead my Community Action Plan project. It was a privilege to be a part of the Professional Women's Group.

Table of Contents

Foreword

Having read the text, assessed the general set up of the ideas that are planned I have come to the conclusion that this challenging project is most likely to come to the fruition it deserves.

The whole text is expressed clearly and with circumspect attention to various points, the appearance of possible obstacles, and even at this early point the text develops ideas about concerning the potential venue to insure stable, smooth and definite development of the project. It was prepared with obvious care, with clear eyed vision regarding its targets, as well as the obstacles that might be encountered. To seek the advice of mentors, who would assure the values and moral basis of the project is another worthy part of the general plan to be pursued.

A further important point is the involvement of the community as well as the input of committed volunteers who would be able to assess the challenges and be inevitably involved in carrying out the various stages of the project successfully. What is most important is the fact that volunteers will be a substantial part of the project. They are bound to bring in energy and enthusiasm.

The plan to initiate workshops will make it possible to receive feedback which in turn will assure the general practical and theoretical value will be aired and discussed. The way the whole plan has been set up, is admirably clear and weighs the potential values and targets with clear eyed energy and obvious intelligence. The plan also involves exploring assessment of the various aspects of potential research to be carried out, including budgetary needs, checking documentation and tracking the development of workshops. It shows awareness of the budgetary needs of the project and pays attention to problems of distribution.

All this shows clearly the careful and thoughtful process of the creative and practical ideas that have gone into finding and clarifying ways to develop this challenging project that promises to be of lasting human value.

Marketa Goetz-Stankiewicz
Professor Emerita
University of British Columbia

Synopsis

When I decided to create my Community Action Project, I never imagined that I would be a recipient of 2018 Community Champion Award and 2019 Caring and Safety Award for all my volunteer contributions and for the impact my project Nutrition on a Budget: Eat Well, Feel Better made within the community.

This book is a blueprint filled with tips and tools I used to build my successful project. The information covered within this book is relevant, meaningful, and practical. I hope it will inspire you to become the next Community Champion!

Creating a successful Community Action Project can be an intimidating task but it does not have to be. It begins with an idea and commitment.

Having built my career by successfully managing multi-million dollar operations, I earned a reputation as the "backbone of the business" from my clients and peers. Seeing the success, I made by handling other people's projects, I decided to step out of my comfort zone and create a project from scratch to help my community. What

I envisioned was a healthy world where women, families, and individuals faced with financial constraints can learn at no cost, how to access and maintain a balanced/nutritious diet while on a limited budget. I soon realized that I would have to navigate a stream of obstacles and fears in order to make my project successful.

I took my vision and put it into a series of actions that ensured the project was relevant, practical, achievable, and most of all – helpful to the community.

During the development stage, I faced several obstacles, including an important cancellation, leaving me with a difficult decision that could impact the success of the project. Tenaciously, I faced the obstacles as they came, motivated by the vision of what I aspired to achieve for the greater good of my community, never realizing that while on this journey to help others I was also working on my personal growth.

My keen commitment and integrity brought the project's seed of a vision into reality where a committed group of grateful participants faithfully attended the entire series of workshops and gave the program very high reviews.

Introduction

Do you have an idea for community change but do not know where to start? Maybe you are wondering if your idea 'fits' into the definition of a Community Action Project?

A Community Action Project (CAP) is a project that can be initiated by anyone who wants to make a positive change within their community. By creating a CAP, you can raise awareness, address issues, connect communities together, empower people to make a change, shift focus and gain momentum to make a difference.

Creating a CAP from scratch can be nerve-wracking and intimidating at first. Especially when this is your first time creating it. Ground yourself, and be present in the moment. It is important to understand that obstacles and challenges will arise. With a clear mindset, you can take control of any situation and conquer any obstacle.

Remember to breathe.
Everything begins with a seed of an idea.

That being said, let me ask you this:

- Do you have an idea or a vision for a project that can benefit your community?
- What is it that you want to accomplish?
- What do you want this project to deliver?
- How would the community benefit from your idea?
- Who would fund this idea or where can you get the money for it?

Write down your thoughts and answers.

_____

_____

_____

_____

_____

_____

_____

_____

Then ask yourself, how committed are you to this challenging yet thrilling new endeavor? Are you willing to do whatever it takes to bring it to fruition? Are you prepared to face your fears?

I raise these questions because many do not realize how much work and time investment it can take to bring a successful project to fruition.

Maybe you are already asking yourself, how do I begin building a CAP? Where do I start?

I will answer all of these and other questions I came across while building my project. I will share insights and obstacles to anticipate and avoid. This book offers useful tips, tools, and resources you can use to build your project. As you follow along, you will also notice that this book is designed in the form of a step-by-step guide that can help you through the process of creating your own new community project.

Now, let me tell you a bit about my story and how I got involved in creating a CAP project. I have always been a bit of an overachiever. I knew that I wanted to make a difference within my community. Volunteering for other organizations was not enough, I wanted to do something different, personal and bold. First, I thought about creating a charity organization but I did not know where to start.

Then, as I let time pass I thought what if I created a project?

However, the question: "How do I begin?" kept on lingering.

Finally, one Saturday morning, during a Dress for Success Professional Women's Group (PWG) meeting, the organization that I was a member of at the time, and opportunity to create a community project was announced. To be able to do this, I had to apply to become a PWG Delegate. What is a PWG Delegate? It is a member of one of the Professional Women's Groups, chosen by Dress for Success to represent the organization. Each delegate has to agree to commit their time and effort for a period of one year, and create a CAP project that will benefit their community. Delegates are chosen annually.

This was the opportunity I was waiting for. I submitted my application and within a few months, my application was accepted along with several other PWG candidates from around the world.

We were warned in advance not to choose a topic for our CAP projects because the theme of the project was going to be announced to us once we arrived in Phoenix, Arizona for the 13th Annual Dress for Success "Success Summit", a 3-day women's leadership conference.

This specific event was called 2017 Pow"H"er Influencers Success Summit. Being at this event with 56 other delegates from around the world was an extraordinary experience. The work that Dress For Success does for women world-wide including providing professional wardrobe and other types of resources empowering women's professional and personal growth – it is inspiring to say the least. While at the leadership event, we listened to many different speakers as they shared their stories of low points in their lives and their rise to success. Their stories of resilience were powerful and inspiring. As we listened, we gained motivational tools and information guidelines to help us with our project development.

The theme for everyone's CAP project was announced as "Women in Poverty". Did you know that 1 in 7 women live in poverty or that 56% of underprivileged children live in families headed by women? Women work two-thirds of the world's working hours but earn only 10 percent of the world's income. They own less than 1 percent of the world's property. These were some of the alarming statistics that Dress for Success World-Wide shared with us.

In addition to the "Women in Poverty" theme, we were provided with several subcategories to choose from. After the three-day event was over, we returned home to begin working on our CAP projects.

I had several ideas but narrowing it down and choosing which one to put into action was a challenge. I found myself asking again, how do I start? What I found interesting was even though I am capable of successfully handling any type of high clientele and their projects, I seemed to hit a brick wall when it came to creating my own from scratch.

Passion is an important ingredient for success when working on any project or business venture. Thus, I asked myself what is it that I am passionate about? I love working out and being active. Nutrition and having enough energy to do what I love is very important but how do I incorporate this information into my community project?

I often heard people in the community express concerns that having access to nutritious food is difficult because it is very expensive. Experiencing firsthand how costly nutritious food is at our local grocery stores helped me relate with members of my community.

This gave me an idea to choose the sub-topic of Nutritional Assistance for my project. To get this idea narrowed down into more specifics, I asked myself the following questions:

1. What is it that I wanted to accomplish with my project?
2. How do I see this project playing out? What is my vision?
3. How much time am I willing to spend on this project overall?
4. What tools and resources would I need to make this project happen?
5. What actions do I need to take to make it be successful?
6. How would I feature and advertise the project?
7. What obstacles do I foresee and how do I deal with them?

These questions are definitely thought-provoking. Let these questions resonate with you for a moment.

Write down your thoughts as you think about the above questions.

_____

_____

_____

_____

_____

_____

_____

_____

_____

_____

_____

_____

_____

_____

_____

_____

_____

_____

_____

_____

_____

_____

_____

_____

These questions helped me navigate through the initial nerves of building my first community project from the ground up, and what came next was simply remarkable.

As we move to the next stages of the process, be sure to have pen and paper ready to make notes.

Chapter 1

Chapter Recap:

Idea > CAP Proposal > Self-Care > Tips

Idea

As Earl Nightingale once said, "everything begins with an idea". Whether you already have a project idea in mind or you are starting from scratch, it is important to pinpoint what it is that you want to accomplish. What is it that you want to create? Give yourself some time to think about this. The more specific you get, the better. Write it down in a diary or a journal. Visualizing can help you create a roadmap for your project.

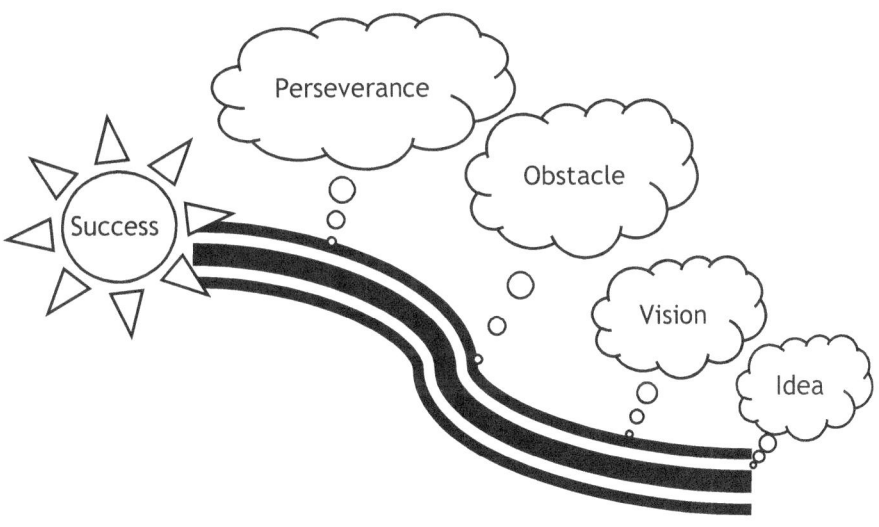

It can also help to ensure you do not miss anything. The mind can sometimes get overwhelmed with thoughts and ideas. It is best to write them down and vet them one by one.

As you go through your ideas, think about how you envision this project working. This might be one of your reoccurring questions throughout the project. Remember, as your project develops your vision of it will evolve as well. It is a normal process.

_____

_____

_____

_____

_____

_____

_____

_____

_____

_____

_____

_____

_____

_____

_____

_____

_____

_____

CAP Proposal

If you are creating a CAP project on behalf of an organization, a CAP proposal plan will likely be required to pitch your idea for approval. Before you begin, make sure you obtain a clear understanding of the organization's expectations, commitment requirements, time investment into this project, fundraising and progress reporting.

Find out if any budget or other types of support will be provided to you to build the CAP. Ask as many questions as necessary to get the information you need to create an effective CAP proposal. Depending on the organization, a one-page document may be sufficient for the initial CAP proposal to introduce your idea.

That type of document should include:

- The goal of the initiative
- Challenges and benefits
- How the initiative will be achieved
- If workshops are included – what topics will be featured
- A description of the need for this initiative and why
- Target audience and expectations

In case a more detailed proposal is required, you can create a report style CAP proposal that will include:

- Title Page
- Table of Contents
- Executive Overview
- Introduction
- Statement of Need
- Initiative Goals
- Objectives
- Methods and Strategies
- Action Plan
- Budget
- Evaluation of the Project Success
- Conclusion

This should be easy to create once you address the above-listed points. When your CAP proposal is approved, you can begin taking steps to turn your idea into action.

Self-Care

It is important to note that when working on a project, the time spent on building, maintaining and running it is as important as setting the priorities straight. Make sure not to overcommit yourself. The project cannot truly be a success if you are too drained to see it through.

When I started my project, I knew that what I was planning to do would require a huge time investment. Fundraising was a huge part of the process needed to achieve the targets I had set out to meet. From previous experience, I knew this would take up a lot of time.

Therefore, I needed to plan things carefully to avoid burnout or over commitment and failure. To do this, I made my priority list and broke tasks down into daily actionable items with approximate timeframes as I worked full time and volunteered at several community organizations. As I went down my lists, I would cross out the completed items and keep on moving forward.

Tips

Tip #1:

If you want to make this project happen and become successful, your commitment to it is essential. Follow through with it – no matter what it takes. Many times, I have heard people say they will do something and then their plan or their project falls through the cracks because other commitments were given greater priority.

Tip # 2:

Be open to feedback and actively listen. If you are working with a partner, it is important to note that similar to any business venture, partners may not see eye to eye. When discussing plans and ideas together try to use "yes and…" instead of "ok but…". This will help you build ideas instead of creating conflicts with each other. Keep moving forward.

Tip # 3:

Mentors are a huge benefit to have. It can be someone you trust, who is supportive, willing to listen and will help you track progress with your project. This person will give you constructive feedback to help achieve your project objectives. During my CAP, a mentor was supposed to be assigned to help me with my project. However, I did not get one until it was too late. My project was already created and successfully actioned. This mentor was long distance and not required at that point. Having a mentor locally would be more valuable and efficient. Also, finding a mentor early is a great idea.

As my project was beginning to launch, a dear colleague of mine, Lisa Stephen, became my mentor. Lisa is a phenomenal facilitator and a huge community contributor. She was very supportive of the value of this initiative and was an extraordinary blessing to have during my CAP journey. After my CAP was built and the workshops were about to start, I was able to share my thoughts, ideas and struggles with Lisa which helped me work through the challenges. This is why I would definitely recommend having a mentor during your CAP project.

Tip #4:

Core values are guiding principles that will keep you in check when things become difficult. It is a great way to keep you accountable and will help keep you motivated when you face obstacles. My core values are promise, respect, integrity, commitment, accountability, and passion. These values are what help me stay on track no matter what challenge I face and they helped me elevate my project to have an even deeper impact.

In conjunction with your values, define your project goals. Are they SMART goals – specific, measurable, achievable, realistic, timely? (Dorian, 1981) Clearly defined goals are important pieces of the puzzle. They will be easier to follow and make actionable. Following your project goals will help keep you in line to achieve successful completion of the project.

Tip # 5:

It is easy to get carried away and look at ideas and obstacles from the boxed perspective. Sometimes it appears to be the easiest thing to do. Believe me, the box perspective is very limiting and it will not bring you the success you want. Thinking outside of the box is more invigorating. Approach your idea from many different points of view and you will be amazed by the flow of information you can obtain.

This approach can also allow innovation and collaboration to come to life.

In case you do end up feeling stuck and you cannot move forward, ask yourself what you already know about your project. Review it in your mind. What is your goal and how will you going to accomplish that? Allow yourself the time to visualize your answers. Make sure you have pad and paper ready to take notes.

You can do this with a cup of tea or a coffee if that will make things easier for you. As you mindfully take a sip, for each answer that you come up with, probe it further for more information. Do not allow frustration to take control. You will be surprized with the flow of solutions that will naturally come to you.

Chapter 2

Research

Now that you have an idea and know your project goals, it is time to conduct research. Research can be done in many ways:

- Online
- Talk to family members, friends, neighbors, coworkers
- Informational interview of various businesses and community members
- Create an online poll or survey and share it on social media

Gather people's opinions about your project. Gauge their reactions. Be prepared to listen actively. Know that some will have different opinions or may not agree with your idea. Do not take it personally, you are only collecting information at this stage to ensure your idea is relevant, actionable and not a repetition of an already existent project.

For example, to narrow down my project idea, I spoke with my family, friends, coworkers and various members of different communities. During these interviews, I noticed the topic of nutrition and low incomes becoming a reoccurring theme. This led me to probe for more information in order to narrow down what it was that the communities really needed?

Once the research is completed, it is time to regroup and review the information obtained. Look for validity, do a SWOT (strengths, weaknesses, opportunities, threats) analysis. (Wikipedia, 2019)

Have you thought of what kind of services your project will provide? How do you see those services delivered? What are the hours or the time frame these services will run? Will there be a cost associated with your services?

In my case reviewing research information enabled me to expand nutrition and low budget ideas into a vision of what I would like to accomplish. This research also helped me identify potential targets and obstacles. It helped me identify a basic plan of what I wanted to accomplish and once I gave it some thought an idea for a project title derived from it. My project title was "Nutrition on a Budget: Eat Well, Feel Better".

Now it is time to think about your project title. What would you like your project title to be? - Make it catchy.

As the research stage grows, you will notice that your goals and project objectives will shift. That is a normal process. Make sure you are keeping up with your journal.

At first, the goal of my initiative was to create a program that would help women who are facing financial challenges to address access to nutritional products while being on a limited budget. The research showed that there is a need for education regarding nutritional meals, to improve participants lives and overall well-being. Initially the intended target were female participants who were struggling financially and might be making poor dietary choices. Then I decided to broaden my intended target to include anyone that was facing above challenges because these participants are often facing numerous health challenges associated with improper food consumption. Organizations that support participants who have financial challenges, for example the Food Bank, were offering mostly non-perishable items such as canned meals and processed foods which contain very little nutritional value.

After the research, I felt that the project needed to evolve to offer other types of resources that would empower participants and their families to change the way they look at food. I wanted to enable them to utilize new tools and resources to incorporate well-balanced meals into their daily diet. The research also identified that clarity about nutrition was required as there is too much conflicting information out there from various sources that make understanding nutrition very confusing, frustrating and contradicting.

As you can see, the more extensive the research is, the better the chances are for the project to grow. Keep track of your research. It will be a useful tool to refer to should updates need to be made. You can keep a diary or notes in a journal, use Evernote, or you can create an MS Word or Excel document and keep all your efforts, dates, contacts and responses saved there for easier access.

Being organized = less stress.

Budget

Let's talk about the budget. Do you have a budget for your project? This is a very important question. It is a factor that will drive how much work will need to be put into fundraising, saving, accounting, spending, etc.

My suggestion is to create a budget report where you will keep a record of all money and donations coming in and out. As you know donations can be given in many different forms. You can use MS Excel for this or any other type of accounting software you are familiar with. I prefer MS Excel as it is workable and easy to use no matter whether one's skills are at the beginner, intermediate or advanced level. Below is one of the examples the budget report can look like.

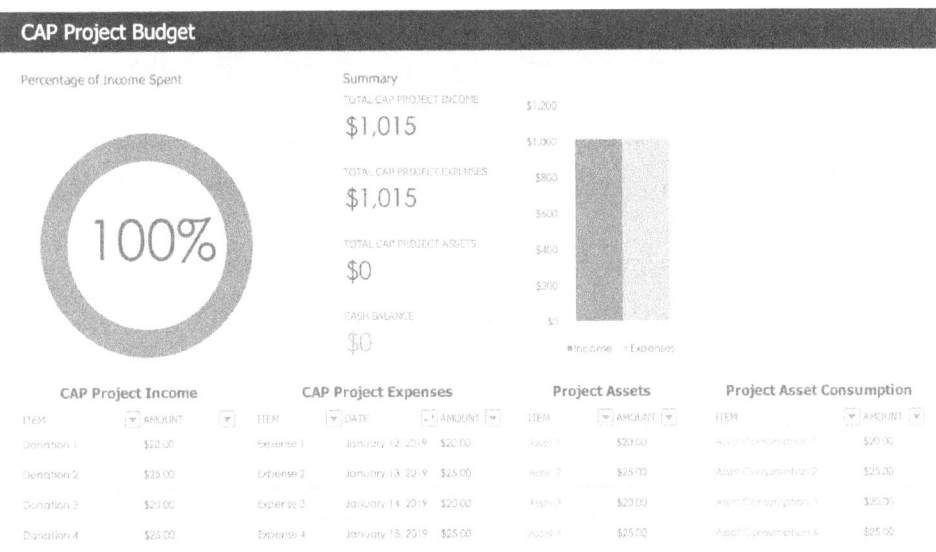

Make sure you keep this report current and accurate. In this report, you will need to keep track of all your expenditures such as printing materials, room cost, food, beverages, incentives, learning materials, honorariums for guest speakers, etc.

When I started building my project, I had no capital to begin with. I was supposed to receive starting capital for my project; however, that did not become available until two weeks after the project had already begun. It was a slight setback but when you allow yourself to anticipate these types of obstacles it is easier to deal with them. Thus, my advice is to always plan ahead.

This set back was resolved by spending some money of my own as well as contacting organizations to request donations in order to achieve my project goals. I would recommend starting to look for donations early in a project. Collecting donations can be an ongoing process.

Fundraising

How do we request donations? In order to approach organizations and local businesses for donations, a donation letter will be required. Donation letters are typically one page long and need to clearly outline what you are trying to achieve with the project.

Make it short, sweet and to the point. If you are not good with words, there are many ideas for donation letters available for free online. You can also obtain it in book format from a library or book stores such as Chapters. Once you find the one you like, make it personable to your project.

Next, I would suggest making a distribution list of target locations you want to approach. Print the letters and distribute them to those contacts on your distribution list. Staples Business is a good place for printing letters, brochures, business cards, and educational materials at a low cost.

Tip: many businesses might give you a slight discount on their services when you tell them that what you are printing or buying is for a charitable cause or project. Be prepared to show them what your project is about.

Your network contacts can be a wonderful source to consider for your project fundraising. Each donation received needs to be carefully logged into your Budget Report. Break it down to ensure all events will be equally covered and supports delivered appropriately as per the program plan.

Create business cards with your project information and hand them around when talking to people about your project. MS Word is a wonderful tool for this.

Have you thought of a logo design for your project? Do you know how your project pamphlet will look? It can be a single page, single fold, trifold or perhaps some other type of a format. It is a good time to start thinking about it.

For my project I used both single page and trifold brochures. Single page pamphlet is great when posting about your project on social media, advertising at various coffee shops, community boards, recreational centres, libraries and so on. Trifold brochures are perfect when handing them out in the community, at the events and reaching out to different organizations.

Personalize your brochures and advertisements for the project by creating unique designs. You can use Canva, Photoshop or MS Word to create different types of designs. MS Word has many different styles available for brochures, business cards and other types of advertisements. Pinterest has a lot of great ideas that can inspire you. When creating a detailed project brochure or an advertisement, you will need to know which services will be provided in order to feature it. When (dates and times) and where (location) is also important. If you do not have this information already figured out, build your designs and save them. You can always update them once this information becomes available. Having them prepared at this stage will save you time creating it later.

In my situation, before I could breakdown the time and location for the services I was planning to provide during my project, I had to figure out the venue. This is why I used one-page pamphlet to advertise upcoming project until the venue was secured.

Advertising

To advertise the project, you can use various social media platforms such as Facebook, Twitter, Instagram, Pinterest. Create a project blog, post regular updates, pictures and upcoming events there.

Keep it going and maintain it regularly. On your Facebook page or a blog, make sure to post the synopsis and mission statements as that will capture the readers' attention. Ask your family and friends to share your project posts. Advertising can also be done through free local community news outlets (online and in print) as well as through paid advertising services and newspapers.

Another cool feature you may consider is creating a brief Prezi presentation about your initiative. Instead of saving it on the USB drive and carrying it with you, Prezi creates a website link for your presentation which you can easily share with your network connections as well as your community targets. This easy to use program has many added features to make your presentations stand out. It will also deliver a clear message of what your initiative is about and what support you are looking for.

During my project, I used Prezi presentation while doing public speaking seminars about the upcoming project to encourage volunteers and donors to join my CAP.

Be sure to have copies with you of your project's pamphlet with your contact information and a brief snapshot of your project objectives. You can hand them out to the audience during your CAP presentation. I would also suggest including these to your donation letters. Distributing letters in person is a great way to make contacts, build first impressions and network connections. If there are places where you are unable to drop off the letter in person, I would suggest mailing or emailing it and then following up with a phone call a week later.

I know that asking people and businesses for contributions can be nerve-wracking. If you are an introvert like me, hang in there. For me, the toughest thing was to ask for donations but once I saw how organizations such as my employer were keen on supporting me, I realized that others also saw the value of what I was trying to accomplish for my community.

This gave me the boost I needed to keep asking.

Be prepared to face your fears, to get out there and do what needs to be done to make your project successful.

The communities are counting on you!

Progress Report

Believe me, seeing everything come together, having various community members step up to support my initiative - to make it possible for the participants to receive the clarity, resources, and learning tools they needed in order to eat better and thrive - was remarkable.

Get to know your community. Attend various community and networking events, spread the word about your project. Ask your contacts to do the same. As you do this, keep track of all your activities.

You can create a Progress Report in either MS Word or Excel where you can document all your actions. Make sure you keep it current.

This type of report is a helpful and organized way to track your follow-ups. It will allow you to see who you have already contacted, when and what their responses were. You will be able to sort it and prioritize your next moves.

Especially when it comes to donation letters, much like proposal letters or job applications, follow up is extremely important.

#	Activity	Initial Contact Date	Contact Outcome	Follow Up Date	Progress Notes
1	Developed Idea for CAP Project	Date	-	Date	Brainstorm further CAP idea ... What do I want to accomplish? What's my goal?
2	CAP Project Community Research	Date	Plan made for community research - identify community needs	Date	Target area identified
3	Document Research Review Outcome	Date	-	Date	Document research progress, categories explored and the challenges faced identifying CAP subcategory
4	Review research and brainstorm further	Date	-	Date	Identified resources needed for the project, plan of execution made regarding contacting the community resources
5	Created CAP Plan and first draft of CAP brochure	Date	-	Date	Updated CAP plan and completed CAP brochure
6	Loblaws	Date	Contacted Re: Donations, Voucher Support	Date	No response received to this date
7	Created donation letter and identified community contacts for fundrasing	Date	Received positive response quickly from ABC Committee with offer of sponsorship - requested to follow up closer to the date and let them know what type of support is required	Date	Followed up with ABC Committee organizer, $500 Donation confirmed
8	Reached Out to Dream Program for Support	Date	Received encouraging reply + was introduced to several of their community networks	Date	To follow up via phone call with Program Manager in a month.
9					
10					
11					
12					
13					
14					

Chapter 3

Chapter Recap:

Venue > Community > Synopsis & Mission Statements > Volunteers > Workshops

Venue

The venue is a very important factor as it often dictates the length of the project especially when funding is limited or is not available. This can be one of the first obstacles. My venue objective was to have the entire project facilitated at the same location to ensure easy access and stability for participants. Stability and location are important factors for successful attendance. The questions I would suggest asking are:

- Is the location accessible?
- Is it big enough to accommodate the setting the project requires?
- Is the timeframe of the venue availability feasible for participants to attend?
- Will there be a conflict with any other loud event happening at the same time?
- What are the costs associated with it?

If your budget is small you probably wonder how to obtain a venue without any funds.

Well, this is similar to fundraising. The key is to reach out to various businesses. I recommend talking to Libraries, Cultural

Centers, Banks, Community Centers, and other organizations. Ask them if they have a room available for your community project. Keep in mind that some businesses will want to ensure your project objective is aligned with their mission and values, especially if you are looking to obtain the room at no cost. You may also run into individuals who may not want to invest in the project without being shown proven assurances that the project will be a success.

I also encountered businesses that refused to contribute to my project because they felt they would not receive a huge media presence. That is okay. They may not have seen the value of what I was trying to accomplish but other organizations did and that is all that matters. Do not let rejections be a deterring factor. Keep moving forward! There are many organizations out there eagerly awaiting to support new community initiatives.

If you chose to look for a venue at a cost, make sure to look back at your budget and see if the cost will be feasible. Sometimes venues can be the most expensive part of a project's budget. This is why it is important to assess and plan carefully. Take all foreseeable expenses into account before deciding how much to pay for the venue. Community Centers and Banks such as Vancity often offer their rooms free of charge for new businesses and community projects. It is their way of helping the community. Community centres can also feature advertisements about the community project in their event catalogues as well as at their centres and they typically will take care of the participant registration process. Be sure to ask about that.

Once the venue has been successfully booked, it's time to put the final touches on the plan for deliverables, whether it is for workshops or other types of community engagement. Keep in mind that the venue can sometimes put a twist into your project schedule especially if the room is only available at a specific time (i.e. 0730hrs or 1900hrs), time length (i.e. one hour per day) or duration (i.e. one or three months).

The venue that was secured for my community project only accommodated ten sessions over a span of three months. The room was available only on Monday evenings from 1900-2100 hours. Therefore, I needed to design the curriculum in a series of ten workshops to be presented during this time frame. To capture participants' attention and ensure they would want to commit to attending sessions so late on Monday evenings, I created informative, engaging, interactive content for each workshop. These are some of the things to think about for your own project.

Community

For my CAP, I envisioned enlisting other community members to be part of this initiative. Not only as participants who were learning but actually having Nutritionists, Health & Wellness experts and Chefs attend the workshops as the guest speakers and share their knowledge. We all know that knowledge is power but sharing it for a greater good of the community is something extraordinary and priceless.

The fact of the matter is, we all get so caught up in our busy, everyday lives that we forget to prepare meals and eat well. Many people do not know how to meal prep or utilize leftovers to their full potential; therefore, a lot of food is wasted. To prevent this, I knew that clarity and education about nutrition are urgently required, especially for individuals who are already struggling and on a limited budget. What better way to deliver this than by having experts come in and share their knowledge.

I knew that finding these experts who were willing to selflessly donate their time and expertise was not going to be an easy task, but I had to try. For months, I was reaching out to various contacts and community businesses for donations either in the form of their time to share their knowledge or to fund nutritional snacks and incentives for the participants during the workshops. The truth is, not everyone will be willing to contribute. Some are already involved in other initiatives while others will have their own reasons why they do not want to donate. These are all part of the learning experience and research. Some may not see the value of the initiative until the initiative is fully in motion. No matter the reason behind it, we must keep going forward. There are plenty of experts out there willing to make a difference.

As each contact attempt was made, I kept documenting all my efforts and responses in the CAP Progress Report. Follow up, follow up, follow up! It is our responsibility to keep following up to make sure things get done, people are booked and confirmed.

The difference between volunteer vs. paid engagement is that people's priority may suddenly change. You may find yourself in a situation where the speaker will be a no-show or cancel at the last minute. To avoid this before it becomes too late, it is essential to follow up and then confirm prior to, and even on the day of the event. It is also good to have a backup plan, just in case things do not work out.

In my case, the first workshop's guest speaker had confirmed but ended up canceling due to a family issue. The timing was bad. It happened during the December holiday season and it was very difficult to find a replacement - such is life. I must have sent out numerous letters looking for a replacement guest speaker and had received zero favorable responses. It began to look like I was going to present the first workshop myself. As I was getting prepared, I never stopped believing that everything would be all right. With a lot of persistence, hard work, and faith, this obstacle was resolved a week prior to the first workshop session. Registered Holistic Nutritionist, (RHN), Renée Pelletier, walked in and was excited to join this initiative once I told her what I was working on. She was amazing and eager to share her expertise at no cost.

Regardless of the short notice, Renée delivered an invigorating "Nutrition 101" session successfully. All participants were able to learn about nutrition basics, where to shop, what to buy: non-packaged goods vs boxed items, the difference in nutrition between vegetable vs. meat and cheese. Furthermore, they learned how to compare nutrition in foods on a budget, what a calorie is, salmon vs. hemp, and so on.

Renée engaged participants, leaving them astonished, requesting to be added to her mailing list, and asking to have her brought back for another session.

In addition to Renée, I was fortunate to meet and collaborate with several other Nutritionists, Fitness Experts, Paralympic Superstar and a Chef. This proved that my vision of enlisting other community members to be part of this initiative was possible as well as that all challenges can be conquered as long as I believe.

Coworkers and friends can be amazing assets too. I was lucky that the employer I used to work for is extremely involved in the community and has various committees who were happy to support my project.

Project Synopsis & Mission Statement

When canvassing the community for support and advertising of the project it is important to have a synopsis and mission statement prepared because these will help to explain what you are trying to accomplish. Both the synopsis and a mission statement should not be longer than a paragraph.

Here is an example of the synopsis and mission statement I used for my project:

Synopsis: *This initiative was created to help families and individuals from different communities faced with financial constraints to learn at no-cost how to access, maintain balanced & nutritious diet while on a limited budget. The project offered a variety of classes and resources to help, empower participants to learn, improve nutritional intake and overall well-being.*

Mission: *To bring communities together for one very important cause – to provide resources, empower and inspire women to learn at no-cost to access & maintain balanced and nutritious diet while on a limited budget.*

Volunteers

As the workshop proceeded, this initiative inspired participants interest in volunteering for the project. They helped me set up the venue before each workshop began, volunteered to spread the word about this initiative within their communities and collect donations. It was obvious that these volunteers became interested in the success of the project.

Having volunteers is a wonderful blessing because with their support, the program moves along smoothly. Seeing the vested interest and commitment of these volunteers into this initiative, I decided to invite them to become a part of my CAP Committee where they would be able to contribute their own ideas to help grow and improve the project's objective.

This enabled us to continue providing services even after the 10 weeks were over and the venue at the Community Centre was no longer available. Our new mission became to help an outreach group of single mothers who were survivors of violence. We were able to successfully deliver workshops and resources they needed to thrive.

When building your own CAP Committee, add as many reliable members as you would like. Building a community project does not have to be a chore, it can also be fun as long as it keeps up with the initiative's goal and values.

As time passes your passion and progress with the project will become evident to others. For example, the work I did for this initiative inspired the interest of many in this project which enabled the project's growth, uniting participants of various communities under one roof and creating a Nutrition on a Budget community of its own.

Workshops

When scheduling guest speakers, keep communication clear. This helps speakers tailor their presentations in alignment with the planned curriculum.

It is good practice to obtain a copy of their presentation outlines. This will help you with creating advertisements for their upcoming presentations and it will give you the ability to spot any part of the presentation that may not align with the project objective. Having a copy of the presenter's outline and their presentation is also helpful to the presenter in case there is a computer glitch during the workshop session or a backup is required to be provided. It is always good to think ahead and be prepared.

Spend some time with the presenters before scheduling them to get a sense of their passion, the tone and the message they will be sharing. Having an engaging presenter is essential for the participants to feel connected and for the workshop success. In order to address previously identified concerns of the project, I was very careful when selecting the workshop topics and the guest speakers.

Here is a snapshot of what the project included and how the schedule was laid out:

Week	Workshop Name	Notes
Nutrition on a Budget - Eat Well, Feel Better		
Workshop Schedule		
# 1	Nutrition 101	
# 2	Canada Food Guide	
# 3	Vancouver Food Asset Map	
#4	Plant Based Nutrition 101 & Preparing Plant Based Nutritional Meals	
# 5	Sweet and Deadly: a history of sugar and how it affects us	
# 6	Cooking Nutrient Dense Meals & Preparing Healthy Bagged Lunches	
# 7	Mindful Eating & Effects of Stress on Digestion	
# 8	Making Meals Together as Family – Essential Benefits of Eating Together	
# 9	Meal Planning, Dedicated Shopping Lists, Leftovers, Healthy Bagged Lunches	
# 10	Personal Goal Setting, Session Wrap Up & Certification Ceremony	

Having a relevant topic and engaging content is extremely important especially when the workshops are provided free of cost to the participants. Sometimes, when there is no cost associated with an event, the attendance of participants may not be reliable. For example, during my workshops 15-25 people actually attended (some signed up while others did not) meanwhile 35 were registered and 10 of those registrants never attended. The topics from this community project were of benefit to everyone from low-income women, families, and the general population. To demonstrate participant commitment, a single parent was attending the workshops with her son, while others were arriving straight after their work shift ended, or were heading to a night shift right after the workshops concluded.

Having experts share their knowledge and their passion for nutrition helped participants learn, relate and be inspired to make better dietary choices.

These interactive sessions provided motivation for the participants to keep coming back and learn more, encouraging them to ask questions, seek solutions, obtain clarification and utilize resources to improve their lives. With each session, the participants were able to build a network with their fellow peers and guest speakers, which in turn enabled this project to create a community of its own where participants felt heard, trusted and supported.

In addition to obtaining guest speakers, I also continued working on obtaining donations throughout the project. I wanted to resume providing multiple incentives for participants to keep coming back to the workshops and learn. To achieve this, I reached out to many organizations, nutrition stores, grocery stores, and markets.

Organizations such as Back In Motion Rehab Inc., Cobs Bread Suter Brook and FUUD Canada were tremendous supporters of the project. Another extraordinary fact was that FUUD Canada, a brand new start-up company did not hesitate to contribute to my project in the form of tangible donations (meal kits for all participants) as well as to be a guest speaker at a workshop. Often, Starbucks and Tim Horton's will supply beverages as donations for community events.

Another challenge you may come across is a decrease in participant numbers. For one reason or another, participants may choose to drop out of the program unexpectedly. It could be that the presenter was not as engaging as participants would like, or the topic was too dry for them to understand and follow.

Sometimes, a flu season or an illness can be a factor in why participant numbers can decrease. This means that efforts related to increasing numbers of registered participants should never stop. Continued marketing and promotional efforts through various community supporters, coffee shop community boards, social media outlets, the project's Facebook page, etc. can help boost the number of participants. Word of mouth is another great way to advertise the project. My work colleagues shared the program brochures with their clients and network connections which helped me boost the number of participants very quickly.

Having interactive and informative workshops is very important because they enable participants to learn and interact with the presenter as well as each other. In one of the workshops, participants learned that the food assets are places where people can grow, prepare, share, buy, receive and learn about food.

Participants feedback was that the session was very interactive, informative and they got to learn about the resources they did not know existed in their communities. In addition to learning how to look up resources, free meals, shelters, etc. on a map based on four different scenarios, participants used their own scenarios to locate resources they need in their community.

Chapter 4

Participant Forms

If you are planning to take pictures or recordings of the participants attending the project, it is important that you communicate this to the participants first. I would suggest having a Photo Release waiver form drawn up for participants to sign. It can be created in MS Word document format. Google and Pinterest also have many examples available. Here is another example:

CAP Program Name

Photo Release Form

PHOTO RELEASE

I hereby grant _____ (hereinafter referred to " _____ ") permission to use my photograph in all current or future publications, including paper and electronic ads, blogs, website, news, social media posts including and not limited to Facebook, Twitter, Instagram, Pinterest.

I understand that the circulation of the materials could be worldwide and I hereby waive any claims for royalties and compensation of any kind of _____ use or publication of these materials. I understand and agree that these materials are the property of _____ .

I understand that these materials will be used in respectful manner for lawful purposes. I have read this release before signing below and I fully understand the content, its meaning, and impact of this release.

Print Name: _____

Signature: _____

Date: _____
           (DD-MM-YYYY)

Know that some participants may not be comfortable having their picture taken. It's important to respect their rights. I would suggest to hand out the photo release waivers at the beginning of the session. Collect them after they have been signed and save them.

When creating the photo waver, I would also suggest creating a Participant Feedback form. This form will help you gather the feedback about your program, its efficiency and can be used as program testimonials.

There are many examples available online. You can also use surveymonkey.com to create an online feedback form. I would suggest to tailor this form to your participants convenience. In my case, the participants preferred to fill out the paper version of the feedback form while at the workshop because it was more convenient for them. See example on the next page.

Remember to document your project impact and deliverables. It is a gratifying experience to look back and see what you have been able to accomplish!

Participant Feedback Form

Please rate your workshop experience:

The workshops I attended were well-organized

○ Agree   ○ Neutral   ○ Disagree

I am satisfied with the quality of information presented

○ Agree   ○ Neutral   ○ Disagree

The guest speakers were professional and knowledgeable

○ Agree   ○ Neutral   ○ Disagree

The topics were interesting and informative

○ Agree   ○ Neutral   ○ Disagree

I had the opportunity to ask questions

○ Agree   ○ Neutral   ○ Disagree

Rate your overall experience at the workshops

○ Excellent   ○ Good   ○ Fair   ○ Poor

Would you recommend _____ community program to a friend?

○ Yes   ○ No

Comments:

_____
_____
_____
_____

Name: *(Optional)*   **Date:**

_____   _____

Attendance

Keeping track of participants attendance is important step to document and measure project impact and deliverables. This can be accomplished by creating a spreadsheet or MS Word document. Make sure it is regularly updated during the workshop sessions.

You can also use Eventbrite or other type of event calendars for participants to sign up. This can be another way to track the attendance.

By doing so, you will be able to gauge participants commitment to your workshops.

Some venue locations have their own way of tracking attendance and participants signup for events. Feel free to ask them about this service. Utilizing their signup document can be another way of tracking your participants attendance and engagement.

Deliverables

Deliverables are vital step of the project process. They speak volumes about the achievements, the goals, and so much more. When I decided to create my project, I never imagined that the project and I would be recognized or receive awards. Seeing my CAP ranked #4 in the "Top 10 Community Action Programs Worldwide" list by Dress for Success felt surreal. The projects' success was also featured on the Vancouver Dress for Success website for 2018 Community Action Projects, as well as at several media outlets.

In September 2018, the project and I were recognized in front of Parliament and I received the 2018 Community Champion Award.

In April 2019, I received a Caring and Safety award for all my volunteer efforts from the City of Port Coquitlam Council.

The most gratifying experience for me was the fact that my project was able to accomplish all set goals and receive such a wonderful feedback from the participants.

The CAP workshops were able to achieve the following:

- Clarify what nutritious food is and bring awareness about its importance
- Address challenges and benefits associated with healthy eating
- Where to buy nutritional products at economical prices and how to read product labels for nutritional information
- How to research and find nutritional resources and assistance within participants' communities
- How to prepare nutritional meals and to obtain all the nutrients our body requires from a plant-based diet
- How to utilize food to its full potential and prevent food loss
- History of sugar and how it affects us (the diseases associated with its consumption)
- How to cook Nutrient-Dense Meals – to utilize all the fruits, vegetables and other nutritional sources to its full potential
- Mindful eating and the effects of stress on digestion
- Making meals as a Family – Essential Benefits of Eating Together
- Meal planning, dedicated shopping lists, leftovers, healthy bagged lunches
- Personal goal setting, the recap of all previous sessions and storing the food properly to prevent food loss

Having the support of the community vested in the success of this CAP made my experience of building this project abundantly exhilarating and powerful!

Testimonials

The testimonials from the participants who attended the workshops, as well as volunteers, community sponsors, project supporters and the guest speakers are a true reflection of the impact a successful CAP can make on the communities.

They are true and unbiased statements that speak volume about the project, its achievements, your efforts and credibility. These can be helpful when looking for:

- Project funding
- Free venues to host your project
- To attain more participants
- To extend your project duration

I hope this book was able to answer your questions and provide you with useful tools to help you create your own successful CAP. Considering all the challenges I encountered, it was rewarding to see the project have such a positive impact on the participants.

The next page will show the testimonials my project received. I hope they will inspire you to become the next CAP Champion of your community!

CAP Testimonials

"My name is Renee Pelletier, as a Holistic Nutritionist I have been working with Maria Shylov to create some food related educational material and present it to the workshop's participants in Coal Harbour.

Every week there is a good turnout of participants and many of the same faces return week after week. This is encouraging and indicates that they are receiving value by attending each class.

The topics presented are extremely informative, well-structured and organized, and of great value to the majority of the population. There is much nutrition information available today on every type of media, one source will often contradict another source, so to know which source to trust can be very confusing and frustrating.

Maria's workshops have streamlined this process, giving the people an opportunity to get educated by the presenters and trust their information sources. These workshops are interactive, giving participants an opportunity to ask questions which I feel is a tremendous step in building trust with a presenter. The participants have even been given opportunity for feedback on topics they would be interested in learning which lead to the creation of one of my presentations on sugar and diabetes.

Overall, I see that the participants are extremely interested in the information presented. They ask some very intricate questions indicating a certain level of interest and wanting of deeper understanding. This I feel is a true indicator of value and interest.

After I presented the sugar and diabetes topic, I had two of the participants discuss with me my views on completely eliminating sugar from their diets. They are both making plans to eat a sugar free diet in an attempt to eliminate pain, boost the immune system, and reduce inflammation from future scheduled surgeries. This is a big deal. Participants are looking to directly apply what they have learned in the workshops to their lives.

I think overall this workshop series has been very successful. Topics presented, attendance rate and questions asked are all proof of this. It is a pleasure working with Maria, she is kind and passionate and truly wants to be of benefit to the people in her community."

Renee RHN, 604-340-8883
www.reneerhn.ca
Eat with purpose, fuel your mind.

"It has been a real pleasure presenting as an R.H.N. for the series 'Nutrition on a Budget'. I was impressed with the scope of the workshops for the series; planning and vision on Maria's part were evident. I was excited to be invited to speak, and Maria allowed me to choose from any of the weekly workshops and encouraged me to share any nutritional information that would benefit the participants. The participants at my workshop put forth a lot of comments and questions and I think many of these participants have attended most of the series' workshops. I would love to work with Maria again; she was a warm and thoughtful leader and her very well-organized series certainly brought a lot of useful information to the audience. I hope the series receives funding to continue in the fall and possibly in other municipalities."

Patricia Kelly, RHN

"Good nutrition is one of the key components of health. We feel that it's absolutely necessary to educate and empower as many people in our community as possible and teach them about healthy nutrition. Nutrition On A Budget is a wonderful resource to learn, get inspired and grow. Maria's passion and dedication to this project is admirable and we truly enjoy collaborating with her and helping others improve their health and well-being."

Nikki & Zuzana
ActiveVegeterian.com

"I really enjoyed presenting at the workshop. I really loved how everyone was so comfortable and asked questions. Everyone had different experiences and they were able to contribute and made the session much more interactive which I enjoyed. I really think this is a great initiative. You can see this by the number of people coming every week. If you are running this again, please let me know as I really would love to be involved."

Susan Le, RHN
www.susanle.com

"Thrilled to be part of such a meaningful project!"

Thomas and Katie
FUUD Canada

"The CARES program at Back in Motion was delighted to help support Maria Shylov and Dress for Success Vancouver in sponsoring the Nutrition on a Budget series. This series speaks to our core values as well as helping people live a balanced and healthier lifestyle. I'd like to thank Maria and Dress for Success Vancouver for putting together a great series and for helping our community better understand the importance and impact nutrition has on their overall well-being as well as provide them tools to make improvements to their nutritional choices."

Carleen Ferguson
Back in Motion CARES Coordinator

"Cobs Bread has always been about fresh, preservative free products. No added sugars, and no crazy ingredients that you can't pronounce-just great, fresh baked bread. That's why it was an easy decision to be a part of Maria's incredible Eat Well, Feel Better workshops. We understand that access to real food can be limited and difficult, especially on a budget.

However, Maria is showing not only the benefits of eating a nutritious meal, but also that it is fully accessible and doesn't need to be expensive. Maria's passion and enthusiasm regarding her initiative are inspiring. To offer her time for free just shows how committed she is to an incredible cause, and we know the whole community thanks her for continued effort. There's no doubt in my mind that the ripple effect of her workshops are huge- people eating more nutritious meals can mean a better standard of living, mothers and fathers learning to cook nutritious meals means that their children will get the nutrition they need to grow into healthy adults, who will in turn know how to feed their children. It's an incredible cause and we're so proud to help in any way we can."

Alexa
COBS Bread Suter Brook

"I am so proud of Maria! She identified a niche need within the community for information around healthy food choices for people with lesser means, then created an entire program to meet that need. Not being one to dream small, the program included 10 weekly sessions even though she had yet to source who all the guest speakers would be! I have seen some of the challenges that she encountered as she launched this program, and have seen the harvest of success that came from believing in the vision and making it happen. Through all of this, I have also seen Maria's confident excitement take off. She is now forging opportunities to talk with other organizations / contacts to promote hosting this program in additional locations. This program is such a benefit to all – the participants, the speakers as they have another avenue to share their knowledge with people who need it, and the communities they represent. Bravo, Maria!"

Lisa Stephen
Community Project Supporter & Mentor

"I'm happy to identify with this project. Thank you Maria Shylov and your team."

Grace Nwandy Nduagu
CAP Participant

"Nutrition On a Budget Initiative program Maria has created on behalf of Dress Success Vancouver is an amazing program for everyone. Especially the work that Maria puts in to take care of every individual with right path and reminding people about their health is important and precious. This is a great reminder for people who live in a very busy world. I highly recommend this program for everyone!"

Sophia
Community Project Supporter

"Genuinely one of the best workshops I've attended. The guest speakers were excellent instructors, talk was inspiring, informative and the method of delivery was so easy to receive. Adapting new healthy lifestyle is great. I got inspiration from those workshops. Its was great experience new food, recipes to learn I feel really great to attend those workshops."

Arshpreet Kumar
Participant and CAP Volunteer

"I was interested in the Nutrition on a budget from the first time you mentioned the concept at the PWG meeting. I signed up as soon as the registration was open and I looked forward to learning about nutrition and the benefits to my health and budget.

It has been enriching to attend each session. The sessions have changed how I look at food preparation and shopping because it's given me the knowledge and information to make informed choices. The presenters and the content of each presentation has been very helpful. I've learnt about the food map, how to buy nutrient dense food, plant based lifestyles and how to budget. I look forward to each Monday when I get to join the small community created at the "Nutrition On a Budget" presentations. I've found the information very helpful. I've been inspired to make changes to my diet by adding more vegetables and I look forward to each week to learn more."

Yvonne Ramdass

CAP Participant

"Monday nights have become one of my favorite days of the week since I have been attending the Nutrition On a Budget Workshops!! It is refreshing and encouraging to learn about the magic that is food (= I recommend this wonderful program to anyone who is looking to play a more active role when it comes to choosing what you are putting into body daily."

Esther Rose
CAP Volunteer and Participant

"I offered my time to help with the CAP project because I think this project is a great idea. It offers good information and tips about eating healthy and improving eating habits. Especially in Vancouver with the rent being so high, I can see it's challenging for some people to keep that in mind when grocery shopping. During the sessions, the participants feel comfortable to interact and ask questions to the presenters. The sessions are very informative, even myself, I already eat healthy and have a balance diet but I did learned a few things. Hopefully the participants will start adopting new and healthier eating habits. Little by little we can make a difference."

Brenda Comeau
Participant and CAP Volunteer

"The Nutrition on a Budget Facebook page is very informative and always has great topics. I have enjoyed looking at all the articles, wishing I lived closer so I could take advantage of these great classes. The professional speakers covered a range of topics and many looked fascinating. The articles were always colorful and looked great as well as had fabulous information."

Jadine Kohut
PWG Member and DFS Ambassador

"I have enjoyed every session of the Nutrition on a Budget CAP project that I attended. The speakers are interesting and all bring different perspectives and expertise to the group. Maria Shylov is doing an excellent job and working very hard in organizing all the speakers, finishing the workshops on time and enticing even more people to attend by having topic related door prizes and snacks. You are doing an excellent job and working so hard."

Lucia Crosson
Career Services Manager and DFS Vancouver Affiliate

Conclusion

There you have it – an easy to use blueprint for successful Community Action Projects.

In the first chapter, we reviewed that it all begins with an idea which is transformed in the form of a roadmap and explored further to create a vision of what we are striving to accomplish. We covered that personal care and commitment are important in order to prevent exhaustion and project failure. We went over several tips such as having a mentor and creating a set of values and goals to ensure your project success.

In chapter two, we dug deeper to explore an idea and turn it into valuable research that helped us determine what further steps are necessary to grow the project and identify potential targets and obstacles. We also discussed budgetary needs, fundraising, the distribution list and progress report, and the importance of being prepared when promoting the project.

The third chapter covered the essential need for a venue, the benefit of having the community involved in the project, and the impact project synopsis and mission statement have when promoting the CAP. This chapter also reviewed the value of having volunteers involved, the challenges to expect and overcome when running the workshops, the documentation to create to track project performance, participants' feedback and more.

At the end of this book, I have included a checklist and notes section where you can add things relevant to your project and check off your progress as you move through stages.

Remember, we are surrounded by incredible people within our communities who are willing to encourage, empower and support the vision of others looking to make a change, to uplift and help those in need. The people I have come across during my CAP project are a true testament of that!

Now that you know how to create a CAP and have a feel of how astonishing this journey can be, it is your turn to make a difference within your community.

Be AMAZING and keep the momentum going!

CAP Checklist

(✓) Checkmark completed sections as you move through the process of building your project and add any other steps relevant to your CAP:

_____ Project Idea

_____ CAP Team

_____ CAP Title

_____ CAP Proposal

_____ Project Deliverables

_____ Budget

_____ Donations

_____ Venue

_____ _____

_____ _____

_____ _____

_____ _____

_____ _____

_____ _____

Notes

Acknowledgements

I would like to thank all the community members (CAP guest speakers, the volunteers, Professional Women's Group Members, and the community organizations) who took a chance to believe in me and my CAP vision! Thank you for supporting my determination to make a difference in the community.

Lisa Stephen, thank you for stepping in and being my mentor, for believing in my vision and encouraging me to dig deeper. You are a true blessing!

The words cannot describe how grateful I am for everyone's support with my 2018 CAP project.

Dearest Marketa Goetz-Stankiewicz, I appreciate you taking time out of your busy schedule to read this book and your generous review.

Mariana Martin, my life long best friend, thank you for listening to my crazy ideas and always being there for me. Our friendship is a true testament that distance and years apart can never break our sisterly bond.

Candice Critchlow and Jodie McNeice- Thank you both for your friendship, precious time and feedback with this book.

Dearest Nikki Hillman, I loved attending your writers' meet up group and learning from you. Thank you for your time and input on editing my draft.

Book Endorsements

"Maria Shylov created an award-winning community action project that earned rave reviews. Here she offers a step-by-step guide so anyone who wants to make a real difference in their own community can do the same. Written in her naturally encouraging style, this guide is truly an exceptional blueprint for change."

Lisa Stephen, CPRW, CDP

"Maria's genuine desire to help her community and her dedication to health and nutrition made her Community Action Project entitled *Nutrition on a Budget: Eat Well, Feel Better* a natural success. In this easy to follow guide, Maria shares both her successes and challenges in order to pave the road for others to go forward and make a difference. A true testament to the difference one person can make if they just take that first step."

Nicole Cairns,
Community Policing Services Manager

"Maria Shylov delivers an empowering voice guiding readers step-by-step on how to launch a successful community project from a simple idea. A must-read for those looking to make a difference!"

Jason Lee,
Author of Living with the Cat - The 9 Biggest Reasons Why Your Life Sucks!

"As a volunteer coordinator and emergency manager I understand the need for community projects and the benefits that they bring to its members. Deciding where to start is the most difficult step to take. Maria has provided a blueprint on key steps to take when an exceptional idea begs to be brought to life.

This book lists practical solutions to guide its reader into delivering a successful community project and is offered out of the wealth of knowledge that Maria brings from her personal journeys. The passion, dedication and resilient background of this individual is meant to inspire its reader into attaining anything…if only one has the desire to do so."

Tara Stroup,
Emergency Program Officer, City of Port Coquitlam

"Maria is one of the Port Coquitlam more active volunteers. That has given her a great knowledge base to work from. She has seen the good and bad and can help you avoid making those mistakes."

Steve Darling,
Councillor, City of Port Coquitlam

"We are all of service to one another in some capacity. Maria's thought provoking Community Action Project (CAP) will guide you toward implementing sustainable practices in your community to affect a positive change."

Christine Gullacher, BA, Psychology/Philosophy

"I have known the author for several years, and one thing that has always stood out was her dedication to whatever she put her mind to. This book is no exception. Clear, concise, and to the point. This is a must read, as it provides the blueprint to success in any community project."

Kris Gardner,
Occupational First Aid Instructor and Community Contributor

"Maria Shylov has written a must-read guide for anyone considering a Community Action Project. Her attention to detail and thought provoking ideas will stimulate your creative juices!"

Jodie McNeice,
Community Services Volunteer Coordinator -Retired

"Maria is a kind and generous person, who continuously brings positivity and a wealth of experience to projects across our community. Determined to encourage the best in others she has graciously shared her knowledge, helping others build strong community action projects. A leader worth following, Maria has inspired a revolution of kindness!"

Laura Thomas

References

Dorian, G. (1981). There's a S.M.A.R.T. way to write management's goals and objectives". Management Review, 70(11), pp. 35-36.

Wikipedia. (2019, 03 25). SWOT analysis. Retrieved from Wikipedia: https://en.wikipedia.org/wiki/SWOT_analysis

www.ingramcontent.com/pod-product-compliance
Lightning Source LLC
Chambersburg PA
CBHW060652290526
45791CB00012B/1956